The History of Space Exploration

Sequencing Events Chronologically on a Timeline

Greg Moskal

PowerMath™

The Rosen Publishing Group's
PowerKids Press™
New York

In Memory of the Columbia Astronauts

Published in 2004 by The Rosen Publishing Group, Inc.
29 East 21st Street, New York, NY 10010

Book Design: Michael Tsanis

Photo Credits: Cover © NASA/Index Stock; pp. 5, 7, 9, 10–11, 12–13, 19 (background, *Skylab*), 22–23, 24 © PhotoDisc; p. 5 (Galileo Galilei) © Hulton/Archive; pp. 6 (both), 9 (Robert Goddard), 10 (Yuri Gagarin, John Glenn) © Bettman/Corbis; p. 10 (Valentina Tereshkova) © Hulton-Deutsch Collection/Corbis; pp. 10 (*Sputnik*) 11 (*Sputnik* interior) © NASA; p. 14 © Taxi/Getty Images; p. 17 © 1996 Corbis; Original image courtesy of NASA/Corbis; pp. 19 (*Mir*), 21 (both) © AFP/Corbis.

Library of Congress Cataloging-in-Publication Data

Moskal, Greg, 1971-
    The history of space exploration : sequencing events chrono-
  logically on a timeline / Greg Moskal.
        p. cm. — (PowerMath)
    Summary: Gives facts about the history of space exploration,
  from Galileo's telescope to the International Space Station, and
  shows how to use a timeline to organize the information and learn more.
    ISBN 0-8239-8962-3 (Library binding)
    ISBN 0-8239-8850-3 (Paperback)
    6-pack ISBN: 0-8239-7323-9
    1. Astronautics—History—Juvenile literature. 2. Outer space
  —Exploration—History—Juvenile literature.   [1. Astronautics
  —History. 2. Outer space—Exploration—History. 3. Chronology,
  Historical.]   I. Title. II. Series.
  TL793.M6578 2004
  629.4'09—dc21
                                        2002154483
Manufactured in the United States of America

Contents

What's on a Timeline?

A timeline shows dates and events from a period of history. The events are shown in the order that they actually happened. Timelines give us a general idea of what things were like during a period of time by showing a small amount of **information** for each of several events. Soon you will see how important math is when discussing and understanding timelines.

We can learn about timelines by looking at important events in the history of space **exploration** in the order in which they occurred. A timeline about space exploration will show us the dates of key events and discoveries. It will also show us information about important **astronomers**.

This timeline shows events in the life of an Italian scientist named Galileo Galilei. Galileo was the first person to study space using a tool called a telescope. Galileo's telescope used glass lenses to make faraway objects appear closer and bigger.

Galileo Galilei

June 1609	December 1609	January 1610	July 1610	December 1610	May 1612
Galileo makes a telescope based on the invention of a Dutch lens maker.	Galileo studies the Moon.	Galileo uses his telescope to discover Jupiter's four largest moons.	Galileo observes shape of the planet Saturn.	Galileo uses his telescope to observe Venus. He uses his observations to prove that Earth goes around the Sun.	Galileo begins to study sunspots.

Pioneers of Space Exploration

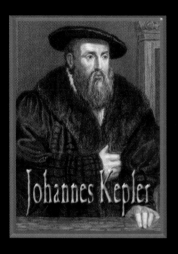

Johannes Kepler

This timeline can help us to understand the discoveries and inventions of some important people who have studied space. Galileo wasn't the only scientist studying our **solar system**. In 1609, a German astronomer named Johannes Kepler used math to show how the solar system worked and how the planets move.

An English astronomer named Isaac Newton used Kepler's work to form his laws of motion and **gravity**. Modern **astronomy** is based on Newton's laws of motion and gravity.

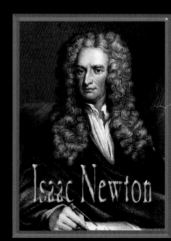

Isaac Newton

We can use our knowledge of math to answer questions based on the information on this timeline. How many years passed between the time that Kepler made his discoveries and the time that Newton published his ideas? To find out, subtract the first year on the timeline, 1609, from the last year, 1687. The answer is 78 years.

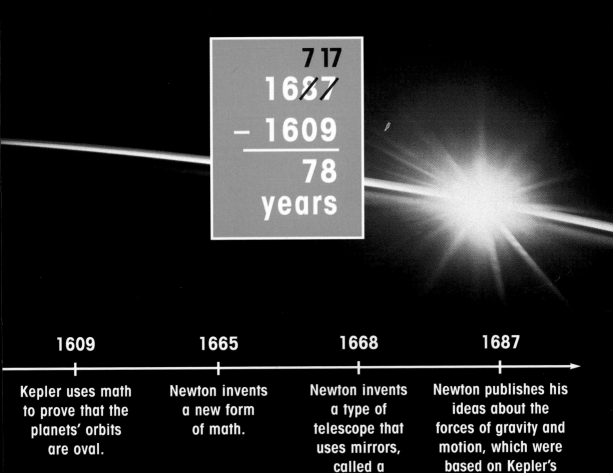

$$\begin{array}{r} {}^{7}\!\!\!\!{}^{17} \\ 16\cancel{87} \\ -\ 1609 \\ \hline 78 \\ \text{years} \end{array}$$

1609
Kepler uses math to prove that the planets' orbits are oval.

1665
Newton invents a new form of math.

1668
Newton invents a type of telescope that uses mirrors, called a reflecting telescope.

1687
Newton publishes his ideas about the forces of gravity and motion, which were based on Kepler's laws about how

A French writer named Jules Verne used his understanding of science to make his adventure stories more believable. Verne's stories about space travel made many scientists want to find a way to travel into space. One of these people was a Russian teacher named Konstantin Tsiolkovsky (tzee-all-KOV-skee). By 1897, Tsiolkovsky had figured out all the basic **equations** needed to put a rocket into space.

The next step was taken by an American scientist named Robert Goddard. In 1926, Goddard **launched** the first liquid-fueled rocket. It reached the height of a four-story building before falling back to Earth. In 1942, a German team of scientists created and successfully launched the V-2 rocket into space.

Study the timeline below. How many years passed between the year that Tsiolkovsky figured out how to send a rocket into space and the year that German scientists actually built the V-2 rocket? Subtract 1897 from 1942. The answer is 45 years.

$$
\begin{array}{r}
\overset{8}{\cancel{1}}\,\overset{13}{\cancel{9}}\,\overset{12}{\cancel{4}}\cancel{2} \\
-\ 1897 \\
\hline
45 \\
\end{array}
$$

8 13 12

1942

– 1897

45 years

1865

Jules Verne publishes a book entitled *From Earth to the Moon,* which makes many scientists want to pursue space exploration.

1897

Konstantin Tsiolkovsky develops the basic equations necessary to launch a rocket into space.

1926

Robert Goddard builds and launches the first liquid-fueled rocket.

1942

A team of German scientists builds and launches the first rocket capable of reaching space, the V-2.

In June 1963, the Soviet Union launched *Vostok 6* into space. *Vostok 6* carried Valentina Tereshkova, who was the first woman in space.

Valentina Tereshkova

John Glenn

Yuri Gagarin

Sputnik 1

This photo shows the instruments inside *Sputnik 1*. These instruments kept track of the temperature and sent radio signals back to Earth.

The Race into Space

Once they had rockets capable of reaching space, the Soviet Union (today known as Russia and other independent states) and the United States raced to be the first country to send a **satellite** into space. The Soviets launched an unmanned satellite called *Sputnik 1* into space in October 1957. *Sputnik 2* was launched a month later. *Sputnik 2* carried the first animal into space, a dog named Laika. The United States launched its first satellite, *Explorer 1*, in 1958.

In April 1961, the Soviets launched the *Vostok 1* with

an **astronaut** named Yuri Gagarin, the first person to go into space. Less than a year later, the United States sent astronaut John Glenn into space aboard the *Friendship 7*.

This timeline shows important dates in the race between the Soviet Union and the United States to be the first country to reach and explore space. We can use this timeline to learn about the early period in the history of space travel. This timeline tells us that the Soviet Union led the early race into space. The Soviet Union was the first country to send a machine, dog, man, and woman into space!

How many years after the Soviet Union launched *Sputnik 1* did the United States launch *Friendship 7*? How many years after the first man traveled into space did the first woman go into space? You can use the timeline to answer these questions.

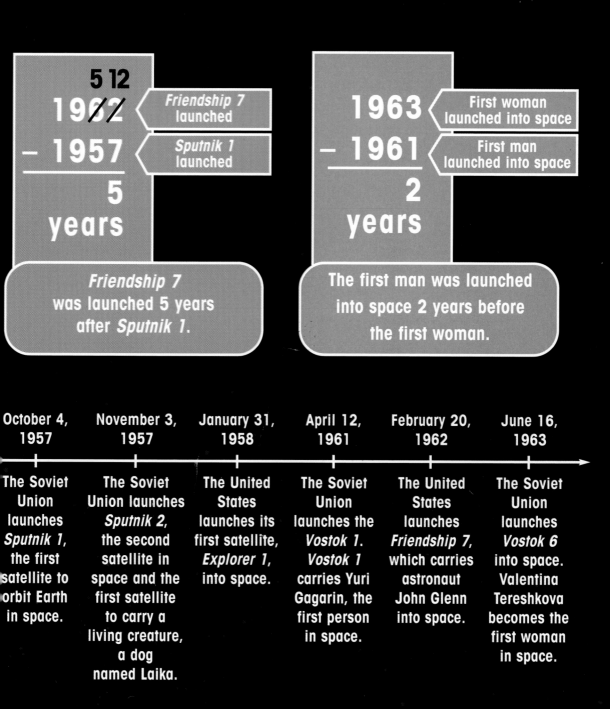

5 12

~~1962~~

Friendship 7
launched

– 1957

Sputnik 1
launched

5
years

Friendship 7
was launched 5 years
after *Sputnik 1*.

1963

First woman
launched into space

– 1961

First man
launched into space

2
years

The first man was launched
into space 2 years before
the first woman.

October 4, 1957	November 3, 1957	January 31, 1958	April 12, 1961	February 20, 1962	June 16, 1963
The Soviet Union launches *Sputnik 1*, the first satellite to orbit Earth in space.	The Soviet Union launches *Sputnik 2*, the second satellite in space and the first satellite to carry a living creature, a dog named Laika.	The United States launches its first satellite, *Explorer 1*, into space.	The Soviet Union launches the *Vostok 1*. *Vostok 1* carries Yuri Gagarin, the first person in space.	The United States launches *Friendship 7*, which carries astronaut John Glenn into space.	The Soviet Union launches *Vostok 6* into space. Valentina Tereshkova becomes the first woman in space.

Let's Go to the Moon

After the Soviet Union and the United States had put astronauts into orbit around Earth, the next goal was to send a person to the Moon. In 1964, the United States became the first country to take close-up pictures of the Moon with a space **probe** called *Ranger 7*.

In 1966, the Soviets were the first to land a probe, *Luna 9*, on the Moon. A few months later, *Surveyor 1* became the first U.S. probe to land on the Moon. In September 1968, the Soviets launched the *Zond 5* probe. *Zond 5* became the first probe to orbit the Moon and return to Earth. It looked like the Soviets were going to win the race to the Moon.

The United States launched seven *Surveyor* probes to the Moon between 1966 and 1968. These probes took close-up pictures of the Moon. *Surveyor 3* was the first probe to actually collect soil from the Moon and carry out experiments on it.

This timeline shows important dates in the race to land on the Moon. The fact that so much happened in such a short time shows how important the United States and the Soviet Union thought it was to be the first country to reach the Moon. How many years passed between the time the United States took close-up photographs of the Moon and the time *Apollo 11* carried astronauts to the Moon?

Compare the events on the timeline on page 13 with those on page 17. When did the United States launch *Explorer 1* into space? How many years after that did the United States send its first space probe to land on the Moon?

The United States won the race to put a person on the Moon. In July 1969, after a four-day journey aboard *Apollo 11*, Neil Armstrong and Edwin "Buzz" Aldrin became the first people to step onto the Moon. Buzz Aldrin is shown here standing next to the American flag.

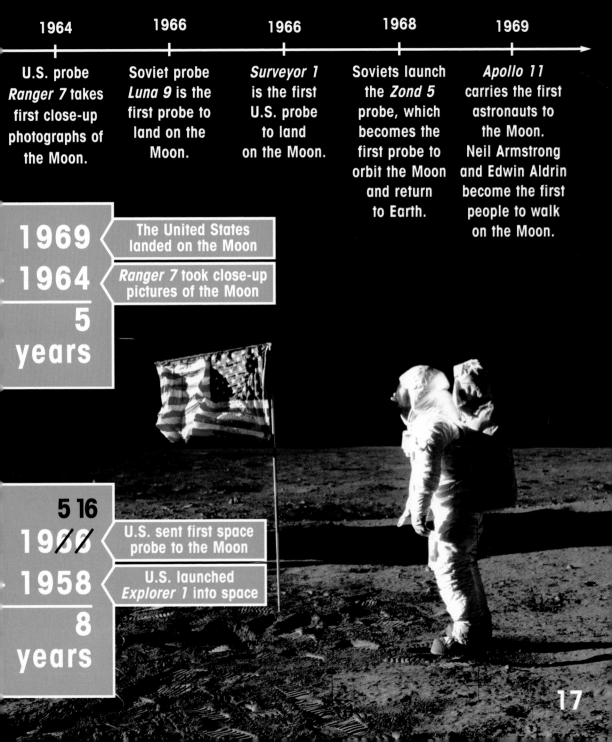

1964
U.S. probe *Ranger 7* takes first close-up photographs of the Moon.

1966
Soviet probe *Luna 9* is the first probe to land on the Moon.

1966
Surveyor 1 is the first U.S. probe to land on the Moon.

1968
Soviets launch the *Zond 5* probe, which becomes the first probe to orbit the Moon and return to Earth.

1969
Apollo 11 carries the first astronauts to the Moon. Neil Armstrong and Edwin Aldrin become the first people to walk on the Moon.

1969 The United States landed on the Moon

1964 *Ranger 7* took close-up pictures of the Moon

5 years

5 16
19~~66~~ U.S. sent first space probe to the Moon

1958 U.S. launched *Explorer 1* into space

8 years

Space Stations

After the race to the Moon was over, the United States and the Soviet Union both built **space stations** to learn more about space travel and how people would be affected by long stays in space. In 1971, the Soviet Union launched *Salyut 1,* the first space station to orbit Earth. The United States launched the space station *Skylab* two years later. *Skylab* was used to do more than 300 experiments in space. Then the United States let *Skylab* fall back to Earth in 1979. In 1986, the Soviets launched the space station *Mir.* The *Mir* space station was in orbit until 2001, which means it was in orbit longer than any other space station.

This timeline shows important events in the history of space stations. How long was *Skylab* in orbit? How long was *Mir* in orbit? We can use this timeline to answer these questions.

Skylab

1979
− 1973
—
6
years *Skylab*
was in orbit

1 9 9 1 1
~~2001~~
− 1986
—
15
years *Mir*
was in orbit

Mir

April 19, 1971	May 14, 1973	July 11, 1979	February 20, 1986	March 20
he Soviet n launches he first ce station, Salyut 1.	The United States launches its first space station, *Skylab*.	*Skylab* falls back to Earth, landing in the Indian Ocean and Australia.	The Soviet Union launches the space station *Mir*.	*Mir* fal to E landing Pacific

The International Space Station

In 1984, U.S. president Ronald Reagan proposed that many countries work together to make a space station to study space and space travel. As a result, sixteen countries helped to build the International Space Station (ISS).

In 1998, Russia launched the first part of the ISS into orbit. Less than a month later, the United States launched the second part. A Russian astronaut and an American astronaut linked the two sections together. Since then, other sections have been added to the ISS. Scientists hope to complete the ISS by 2006 if there are no delays.

This timeline shows important dates and events in the history of the International Space Station. How many years did it take for the ISS to be launched after it was first proposed? If everything goes as planned, how many years after the first part was launched into space will the ISS be finished?

Number of years between ISS proposal and the launching of the ISS:	$\begin{array}{r} 1998 \\ -\ 1984 \\ \hline 14 \\ \textbf{years} \end{array}$	Number of years to complete the ISS:	$\begin{array}{r} 1\,9\,9\,16 \\ \cancel{2006} \\ -\ 1998 \\ \hline 8 \\ \textbf{years} \end{array}$

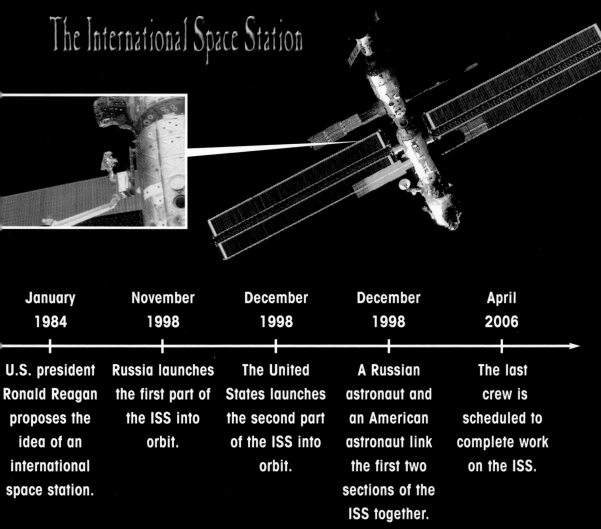

The International Space Station

January 1984	November 1998	December 1998	December 1998	April 2006
U.S. president Ronald Reagan proposes the idea of an international space station.	Russia launches the first part of the ISS into orbit.	The United States launches the second part of the ISS into orbit.	A Russian astronaut and an American astronaut link the first two sections of the ISS together.	The last crew is scheduled to complete work on the ISS.

Using Timelines

The timelines in this book have helped us follow the order of events throughout the history of space exploration. By using our knowledge of math, we can use timelines to find out how much time passed between two or more events Timelines not only show us important dates, they also help us to see how one event may have caused another event. Johannes Kepler's mathematical discoveries made in 1609 encouraged Newton to develop the laws of gravity and motion many years later, in 1687. The work of earlier scientists eventually led to the United States and the Soviet Union sending astronauts to explore space and the Moon. What other subjects could we study with timelines?

Glossary

astronaut (AS-truh-nawt) A person who travels in space.

astronomer (uh-STRAH-nuh-mur) A scientist who studies outer space.

astronomy (uh-STRAH-nuh-me) The science that deals with the Sun, Moon, planets, stars, and other objects in outer space.

equation (ih-KWAY-zhun) A statement that two quantities are equal.

exploration (ek-sploor-AY-shun) The act of traveling to distant or unknown places to discover new things.

gravity (GRA-vuh-tee) The force that attracts space objects to each other and causes planets to orbit the Sun.

information (in-fuhr-MAY-shun) Knowledge given or received regarding some fact or event.

launch (LAWNCH) To send something off with great force.

probe (PROHB) A spaceship that carries tools to record facts about outer space and send them back to Earth.

satellite (SA-tuhl-ite) A machine that orbits Earth in space and is used to study objects in our solar system.

solar system (SO-lur SIS-tum) The system made up of our Sun, the nine planets, moons, and other space objects.

space station (SPAYS STAY-shun) A large spaceship that circles Earth. People live there and do scientific experiments.

Index